POCAHONTAS
INDIAN PRINCESS

BY KATHARINE E. WILKIE

ILLUSTRATED BY WILLIAM HUTCHINSON

FRANKLIN WATTS
London

Franklin Watts Limited
1 Vere Street
London W.1.

SBN 85166 502 0

Contents

The Powhatans

Pocahontas' people, the Powhatans, were Algonquian Indians who lived in what is today eastern Virginia in America. They built villages near rivers and streams on raised land which protected them from floods and gave them a good view of the river. Their villages were usually small, and many were surrounded by a fence of tall poles set close together.

Their houses were wigwam structures, made of upright poles, bent and tied together at the top, which were covered with large pieces of bark or rush mats. In the summer the bark was removed or the mats were rolled up around the lower part of the wigwams to make them more open and airy.

The Powhatans kept gardens in which they grew maize, beans, squash, pumpkins, and tobacco. They also ate wild fruits and berries, nuts, and roots. They fished in nearby streams and were very skilled at hunting bear, deer, and small game.

By the middle of the 1600's, most of the Virginia Indians had been killed or driven off their lands by disease, white men, and hostile Indian nations from the north.

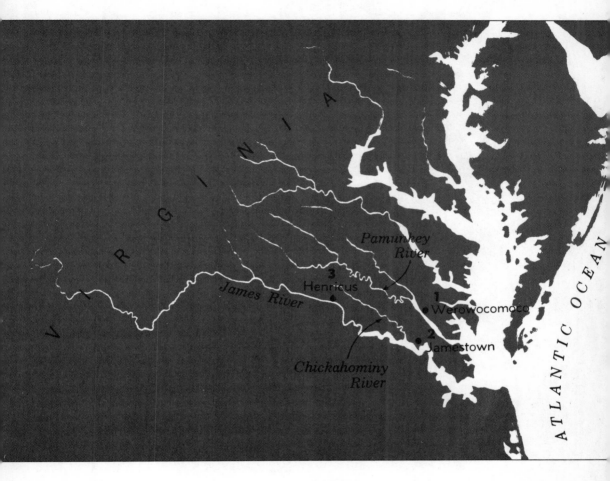

1   Werowocomoco, the village where Pocahontas grew up and where she
    first saved Captain John Smith's life.

2   Jamestown, the English settlement where Pocahontas lived **after being**
    kidnapped and until her marriage to John Rolfe.

3   Henricus, where Pocahontas and John Rolfe moved after their mar-
    riage and where Rolfe grew tobacco.

1

News From the Coast

It was late autumn in 1607. The village of Werowocomoco was uneasy. All summer runners from the coast had brought news about the white strangers who had crossed the Great Water. They had built a fort near the mouth of a river they had named the James.

Twelve-year-old Pocahontas had talked with her father Chief Powhatan about these men.

"They are not Spaniards," he told her. "Spaniards have lived far south of here for many years. These men have lighter skins and they call themselves Englishmen. They came to our shores in three huge canoes with great white wings."

"Are they friends or foes?" she asked.

He shook his head. "I do not know. My brother Opechancanough does not trust them. They have built a village called Jamestown on our lands, and they sail up and down our streams. Their fire sticks spit out flames and make terrible noises. These fire sticks can kill man or beast."

Perhaps Pocahontas should have been afraid, but she was not. She was too eager to see the newcomers.

"I do not fear them," her father went on. "They are human as we are. Their crops did not do well this summer. They were unwise to plant on low, marshy land. Now they want to trade with the Indians for food."

The young girl looked hopefully at her father. "Take me to see the white men," she begged.

Powhatan shook his head. "I am the Great Chief of the Powhatan Indians. I rule over 30 tribes and 200 villages. Let the white men come to me."

That had been months ago and still the white men had not come. Although Pocahontas was disappointed, time passed quickly. She loved life—from morning until night she played, sang, danced, ran, swam in the river, and roamed in the forest. Her name Pocahontas meant The Playful One.

One day she had climbed a tree at the edge of the village and was high up in the branches. Suddenly, through the leaves, she spied a runner coming up the path.

Quickly Pocahontas climbed down and raced after the messenger. As she drew near him, the runner exclaimed, "Take me to Chief Powhatan!" Pocahontas ran along beside him until they reached a long, thatched house in the centre of the village. When the runner entered the door, she slipped in behind him.

Old Powhatan sat with some of his braves on a raised platform at the end of the house. He and his men listened to the messenger.

When the man had finished, the ruler rose to his feet. "Call all my people together," he commanded.

Pocahontas watched the men, women, and children gather.

They grew quiet when Powhatan raised his hand. Pocahontas was proud of her father. He looked every inch a great chief.

"Listen to the message sent me by my brother," he commanded.

The runner stood tall and straight. "I bring grave news," he told them. "There was a battle between the men of an Indian village and a party of the white men. Our people were painted for war. They were armed with knives, bows, arrows, and war clubs. They carried their Okee into battle."

Pocahontas listened excitedly. An Okee was a fierce-looking wooden god covered with skins. It had a warrior's face, bird claws, and savage teeth. The Indians felt it brought them victory.

The messenger went on with his story. "The magic of the white men's fire sticks was too great for the Indians. Many of the warriors were killed, and others were captured. The white men won the battle and ran away with the Okee."

A cry of mourning went up from the people.

"Quiet!" Powhatan thundered. "Let him finish."

"Captain Smith, the white men's leader, sent a brave back to the Indian village," the messenger said. "Captain

Smith told him to see that much corn was brought to the white men. Then their Okee would be returned. The Indians would be paid for their corn with copper, beads, and hatchets. The Indian prisoners would be set free."

Again a murmur went up from the crowd. Powhatan looked less stern.

Pocahontas stole nearer, to her father. She did not fear him, for she was his favourite daughter. "This Captain Smith must be a powerful man," she whispered. "He had won the battle. He did not have to be so generous."

The old chief nodded. "Great men are not afraid to be generous. I shall be generous too. The Powhatans will live in peace with these strangers."

2

Pocahontas and John Smith

The weeks went by, and life went on as usual at Werowocomoco. Then one morning in December another runner arrived with startling news.

"Your brother Opechancanough will be here tomorrow," he told Chief Powhatan. "His men met some white men in the forest. There was a skirmish, and they captured the Englishmen's leader, the great Captain John Smith.

15

Opechancanough is bringing the prisoner to you."

Pocahontas could hardly wait to see the white man. The next morning she put on a beautiful long feathered cape which she wore only at special times. People began to crowd into the house which her family shared with other families.

Suddenly there was a loud shout.

16

Captain Smith was being led in by his
captors.

Pocahontas stared at him. She saw a
sturdy man with a sunburned face. He
had reddish-brown hair and a reddish-
brown beard. His eyes were blue as
the summer sky. He held his head
proudly. Pocahontas liked him at once.
She thought he was the handsomest
man she had ever seen.

B

At first the Powhatan Indians honoured Captain Smith for, among his own people, he, too, was a chief. They brought him mats to sit on. They offered him water to wash his hands and feathers to dry them. They spread food before him.

Then Powhatan's brother began to speak. He sounded angry.

"This white man came up the Chickahominy River into our country. He brought others with him. They killed two of our young braves with their fire sticks. He is the white men's leader, and he must die!"

"The Indians killed two of my men first," the prisoner told him.

"Be still!" Powhatan roared. "I will hear my brother."

The younger chief began again. "I demand his life for their lives."

The Indians nodded. That was their law.

Powhatan raised a hand. "The white man must die."

Pocahontas burst into tears and rushed forward. "Do not kill him," she sobbed.

Her father scowled at her. "His life for theirs," he stated.

The men led John Smith to the centre of the house. They placed two large flat stones one on top of the other. One of them led the prisoner forward. Another forced him to kneel.

"No, no!" Pocahontas cried.

Captain Smith looked gratefully at her. But then a third Indian made him place his head upon the top stone.

"Beat him to death!" Powhatan then ordered.

The guards raised their war clubs. Captain Smith could hardly breathe. He knew that he was only inches away from death.

Pocahontas dashed forward. She threw herself between the clubs and the prisoner. She laid her head against that of Captain Smith.

"I claim him as my own!" she cried.

For a long time no one moved. Pocahontas was trembling in fear. Then Powhatan commanded the Indians to drop their clubs. He looked displeased.

"My daughter has spoken," he growled. "The white man belongs to her, because she has claimed him. It is the custom of our people."

3

Pocahontas
Saves Jamestown

Now Captain Smith belonged to Pocahontas. The other Indian boys and girls looked at him longingly. Each wished that he had a white man for his own.

"He shall play with me—and make bells and beads of copper for me!" Pocahontas told her father.

Powhatan nodded solemnly. "And he shall make me hatchets."

Captain Smith spent many hours with the girl who had saved him from death. He taught her English words. She learned quickly.

"Have you travelled in many lands?" she asked.

He nodded. "Yes, in more than you have ever heard of, for I am a wanderer."

"Where have you wandered?" she asked.

The sun-tanned captain smiled at her. "Oh—to many places. Egypt—Italy—Hungary—Russia."

She repeated the words after him. Her friend laughed at the way she spoke them.

"What is your favourite place?" she asked him.

"London," he told her. "It is a great city in England."

Two days went by. Then Powhatan's guards took the captain to a great house in the woods. They left him there alone. After a while Powhatan himself entered, looking more like a devil than a man. Two hundred Indians were with him. All were painted black.

At last Powhatan spoke. "We are your friends. You now belong to our tribe, and you are my adopted son."

John Smith wondered what would happen next. He soon found out.

"You are free," the chief told him. "You may return to your fort. I ask only a grindstone and two guns in return."

That very day Smith started back to

Jamestown. But first he told Pocahontas good-bye. She called him her English father.

"You are my little Nonpareil," he answered.

"What does that mean?" she asked.

"It means 'Beyond Price,' or 'Without an Equal,'" he told her. "I shall never forget that you saved my life."

Powhatan sent twelve braves to Jamestown with Smith. They were to bring back the guns and the grindstone. Captain Smith did not want the Indians to have guns with which they could attack the settlers. So he fooled them.

"Here are some big guns," he said, pointing to two cannon. The Indians found them too heavy to carry, as he had known they would.

"Would you like to know how the great guns work?" Captain Smith asked. He wanted to discourage the Indians from sending for help.

The gunners loaded one of the cannon with stones and fired it at a tree covered with ice and snow. The loud noise and the flash of fire frightened the Indians. The falling ice and branches frightened them still more. They ran away in fear.

The laughing captain coaxed them back. He gave them simpler presents to take to Powhatan.

Now bad weather set in. Heavy snows fell and wild winds blew. Game was scarce in the forest.

One winter day Pocahontas went to Powhatan. "I would like to take corn to the Englishmen," she told him. "They must be very hungry."

"Do as you please," her father answered gruffly. He remembered that he had not received his two guns. "We have food enough and to spare."

Pocahontas led a long line of Indian girls through the forest to Jamestown. Each carried a large basket of corn upon her back.

They walked more and more slowly as they came to the high log wall surrounding the English village. They had heard of the fearful fire sticks. Only Pocahontas walked quickly.

"The settlers will be glad to see us," she called back to the others.

Still the Indian maidens hung back. Pocahontas called, "Captain Smith!"

The gates of the village opened and a man came out. He carried a gun over his shoulder.

The girls turned and ran. Pocahontas stood all alone.

"I am Pocahontas," she called.

Another man joined the first one. It was Captain John Smith. Pocahontas ran to meet him.

"We have brought you corn," she told him.

Captain Smith seemed glad. "Thank you, Pocahontas," he said. "Some of our people are hungry." Actually many had died of hunger, and most of the others were ill. Captain Smith did not tell Pocahontas. He did not want the Indians to know how poorly protected the fort was.

Pocahontas was speaking again. "We will soon bring you more food," she promised.

"You have brought us an even better gift," the captain said.

"What is that?" Pocahontas asked.

"Friendship," John Smith replied. "God bless you, little Nonpareil."

On her way home Pocahontas repeated to herself what the captain had called her. "Nonpareil—Nonpareil—Without an Equal. I like that."

4

Gifts for Powhatan

During the long winter Pocahontas and her friends returned every week to Jamestown. Powhatan sent gifts of corn, deer, raccoons, and bread. Without the Indians' help, the settlers could not have lasted through the winter.

Pocahontas was eager to see everything in the fort. Her eyes opened wide at the settlers' copper pots and pewter plates. She even tasted the settlers' strange food.

At last warm weather came again to Virginia. More settlers arrived on a ship from England. They, too, needed food.

Other Indians brought food to barter. They traded it for beads, cloth, pins, belts, and other trinkets.

But Chief Powhatan was not happy. Perhaps he was tired of so much trading. Anyhow he wished to trade for tools and guns instead of trinkets. The white men seemed to have too many trinkets and too few weapons. When they next sailed up the river to trade for corn, he would give them only a small amount.

33

One day John Smith and some of his men came to Werowocomoco. This time he did not mention corn. Instead he bowed low to Powhatan. "I bring you gifts from the King of England," he said.

Powhatan looked pleased. "It is good for one chief to honour another," he said.

Captain Smith told the men to bring the gifts ashore. Pocahontas could hardly wait. She loved presents.

Everyone watched to see what the English king had sent. There was a bright scarlet cape, a big wooden bed, a gleaming brass pitcher, a brass basin —and a copper crown.

The chief looked hard at the bed. "Take it to my house," he said.

John Smith's men carried the gifts to

the house. The Indians crowded in to see the strange things. They watched the white men set up the bed. They stared at the feather mattresses and the pillows.

Powhatan's people all laughed and laughed when they learned that many white men slept in such beds. Even stern old Powhatan gave a half-smile.

Captain Smith handed him the gleaming pitcher and the brass basin. Pocahontas, standing by her father, could see their faces in the brass.

Powhatan was a tall man. Captain Smith stood on tiptoe to place the scarlet cape on the Indian's shoulders.

A man stepped forward with the copper crown. "Now you must kneel," John Smith told the chief.

Powhatan sprang back. "I kneel to no man!"

"But a king always kneels to receive his crown," John Smith said.

Pocahontas wanted her father to have the crown, but she knew he would not kneel.

Someone persuaded Powhatan to bow slightly. Then several Englishmen placed the crown on his head, and they all bowed to him.

That pleased the chief. He pointed to his old robe of skins. "Take it to my brother, the King of England," he said.

The Englishmen took the robe back to Jamestown. In time it found its way across the sea to England. It may still be seen in a museum at Oxford.

After Powhatan was crowned, guns were fired from Smith's boats anchored on the river.

"An attack!" Powhatan cried.

John Smith shook his head. "No, the guns are being fired in your honour."

Pocahontas was happy when her father gave a feast for the visitors. There was much food. There was dancing and singing. Powhatan even had a few baskets of corn put aboard the English boats. But they were small baskets. He did not seem to feel friendly, and the Englishmen noticed it.

5

Danger!

Winter had come once again, and Pocahontas was troubled. Her father had begun to hate the white men. She feared he might attack them.

"They have done you no harm," she said.

Powhatan frowned at her. "You are only a young girl. More and more white men keep coming. They move onto our land. They eat our food. They will crowd us farther and farther away from the coast."

One night Pocahontas heard her father as he talked with his braves.

"We will trick the Englishmen. We will kill their leader," the old chief said.

Before long Powhatan sent a message to John Smith. It said: "Send me men to build a house like those at Jamestown. Send me a grindstone. Send me 50 swords, a rooster and a hen, and copper beads. Then I will load your boats with corn."

Captain Smith sent men ahead by land to build the house. Then he led 46 men up the river. They travelled on a sailing boat and a barge.

The weather was bitter cold. The river was partly frozen when they reached Powhatan's village. The men on Captain Smith's barge had to break the ice near the shore before they could reach the land.

They took shelter in a hut on the edge of the village. Powhatan sent them some food, but the next day when they saw him, he was unfriendly.

John Smith asked for the promised corn.

Powhatan stared hard at him. "You must lay down your guns. Otherwise my people will think you have come to make war."

Pocahontas stood by, listening intently. She looked from her father to Captain Smith.

"We come in peace," John Smith said. "We mean you no harm—but we will not lay down our weapons. Now where is our corn?"

Captain Smith did not trust Powhatan. Smith asked some Indians to cut the ice that had formed around his barge. Then he and his men would not be trapped.

Meanwhile Powhatan disappeared. A number of his braves surrounded Smith's hut. This made Smith angry. He fired his pistol and waved his sword. The Indians fled.

A messenger arrived from Powhatan. "Chief Powhatan fled because he feared your guns," the messenger explained. "But even though you carry weapons, he is still your friend. Take your corn and go."

"Powhatan is our friend until we turn our backs," Captain Smith thought.

Soon the corn was loaded on the waiting barge. By this time the tide had gone out. The barge could not be launched. Smith and his men were forced to spend another night on shore.

They returned to their shelter and built a fire. Suddenly from the darkness outside came the cry of a whippoorwill.

Captain Smith sprang to his feet and listened. Then he went out into the night. Pocahontas was standing in the shadows. She had been crying.

"You must leave with your men at once," she told him. "My father plans to kill you. He will send men with food for a feast. While you are eating, they will attack. I beg you to escape now!"

"We cannot leave until the tide comes in," the Englishmen said.

"Then be on guard," Pocahontas warned. "Powhatan's men are already on their way."

Everything happened just as she had said. Soon Indians came with food. They pretended to be friends. But Captain Smith and his men kept their weapons in their hands. When high tide came, they rowed their boats away to safety.

After this Powhatan would not allow Pocahontas to visit Jamestown. As the months passed she was anxious to know how her English father was getting along. She welcomed any news about Jamestown that was brought by scouts to Powhatan.

Finally bad news came. Captain Smith had been seriously injured in a gunpowder explosion. He had sailed away in a ship.

Pocahontas sobbed bitterly. "He has gone home to England to die," she cried. "I shall never see my English father again."

For months she was sad and seldom smiled. She had learned to love her English captain dearly.

6

The Kidnapping

Jamestown suffered from the loss of Captain Smith. He had learned to deal successfully with the Indians.

The winter after Smith left, Powhatan's warriors attacked the fort several times. Some settlers were killed. Many others died from cold, hunger, and sickness.

Chief Powhatan was glad. "Now the white men will leave," he said.

But they did not leave. A governor was sent from England to take Smith's place in Jamestown.

More and more colonists came across the sea. Small settlements had sprung up at several other places. The Indians realized sadly that the white men had come to stay.

During this time Pocahontas grew into a beautiful young woman. One summer when she was grown, she visited the village of a chief named Japazaws.

This chief had been a friend of John Smith. He was also a friend of Captain Argall, who had settled in Jamestown after Smith left. Captain Argall often sailed up and down the rivers to trade with the Indians.

One day he sailed to the village of

Chief Japazaws. He had with him a huge copper kettle which shone in the sunlight. Japazaws and his wife admired it.

Then the captain and the chief went off together. Pocahontas wondered what they could be talking about. Every time she looked up the chief was staring at her.

After a while Japazaws called his wife aside. "Captain Argall will trade us the kettle," he told her. The woman's eyes opened wide. "What does he want for that costly kettle?"

"We have something he wants very much," her husband said.

"What?"

"Pocahontas."

"Pocahontas!" his wife gasped.

"Powhatan is holding some captured Englishmen in his village. He has tools and weapons which his braves have taken from the settlers. The white men want their comrades back. They want their tools and weapons."

His wife began to understand.

"If the white men take Pocahontas prisoner, they could make a trade with Powhatan. He loves his daughter more than he loves his own life," Japazaws explained.

"What are we to do?" the woman asked.

"Get Pocahontas aboard Captain Argall's ship. He will do the rest."

His wife looked at him.

"The white men will not harm Pocahontas," Japazaws insisted. "They will free her when her father returns the English prisoners."

Next morning Pocahontas went with Japazaws and his wife to see the English ship. She was always eager to see new things and new people.

Captain Argall took the three Indians through the ship. When he opened the door of his cabin, Pocahontas entered.

When she looked out the porthole, she saw Japazaws and his wife paddling away. The woman held the copper kettle in her arms.

"Stop!" Pocahontas cried.

The Indians in the canoe did not turn back. They paddled farther away.

She felt a hand on her shoulder. She looked up to see Captain Argall.

"You are my prisoner," he told her.

7

Pocahontas
in Jamestown

"Here she comes!"

The news about Pocahontas had
travelled ahead. The settlers at Jamestown
had gathered to see her arrive.

The Indian girl walked through the
gates of the fort beside Captain Argall.
Her head hung low, and she looked
unhappy.

"It's a shame!" one settler said. "She brought us food when we were hungry."

A handsome young man named John Rolfe stood among the settlers. He never took his eyes off her.

Governor Thomas Dale then stepped toward her. "Welcome to Jamestown, Pocahontas," he said. "We shall try to make your stay a pleasant one."

Pocahontas looked up. "It cannot be pleasant as long as I am a prisoner. I beg you to set me free."

The governor looked a little ashamed. "I cannot do it now, but you shall have your freedom before long. Meanwhile you are our honoured guest."

Governor Dale kept his word. Pocahontas stayed in the home of a leading family. The minister of the

Church of England taught her to read. His wife taught her how to keep house.

But Jamestown seemed strange to her. She had often been there before, but only for short times. Now she slept in a bed instead of on skins. She bathed in a wooden tub instead of in a clear running stream. She ate English food and wore a tight-fitting English dress!

She longed to go home. The governor of Jamestown sent word about Pocahontas to Powhatan. After three months the old chief sent a messenger down the river. His canoe carried seven English prisoners, a few tools, and a small bag of corn.

"Return Pocahontas," the Indian said. "Then Powhatan will send you the rest of the tools and plenty of corn."

Governor Dale sent Pocahontas with many guards in a fleet of boats up the river. When they reached Werowocomoco, two of Pocahontas' brothers greeted her warmly.

But Powhatan was away then, so no agreement could be made. The Englishmen took Pocahontas back to Jamestown.

She seemed almost glad to return. She agreed to be baptized into the Christian faith. The ceremony took place in the little church at Jamestown. The minister said: "I baptize thee Rebecca." From that moment it was her English name.

Pocahontas still missed her father and her people, but every day she missed them less and less.

She now had reason to be happy.

John Rolfe, who had watched her arrive at Jamestown, was in love with her. Pocahontas and John often walked together beneath the trees near the fort.

One day John Rolfe said, "I love you, Pocahontas. I have asked Governor Dale if I may marry you. If he agrees, will you be my wife?"

Her eyes shone with happiness. "I love you, too, John. I will send word to my father. He must say yes before we can marry"

The governor of Jamestown approved the marriage. Deep in the forest Powhatan listened to the messenger who came from his daughter.

For a long time the old chief was silent. Perhaps he was thinking that he was tired of war. He knew that the number of white men was growing all the time. Perhaps it would be better to live in peace with them. Also he wanted his precious daughter to be happy.

At last he spoke. "This is the first time an Englishman has asked to marry an Indian girl. My daughter seems to care for this John Rolfe. I give my consent. This union should mean a true and lasting peace between the Powhatan Indians and the white men."

In April, 1614, Indians and settlers gathered in the little church at Jamestown. They watched Pocahontas and John Rolfe make their marriage vows.

Powhatan had sent a message. He said that he would live forever in peace with the children of the King of

England. If need be, he would move his dwellings away from the towns of his white brothers. His warriors would never attack them again.

Pocahontas and her husband soon went up the James River to live. John Rolfe owned land in a new settlement called Henricus.

At Henricus John built for his wife a handsome house with a second storey. It was very different from the house where she had lived as a child.

John Rolfe grew tobacco on his new plantation and was the first Englishman to do so. Tobacco was a native American plant which the Indians had taught him to grow. The tobacco was shipped to England, where it became very popular. In time tobacco became the largest crop of the colony of Virginia.

The Rolfes' happiness was made complete when their baby son Thomas was born. They often stood side by side, admiring him as he slept in his English cradle.

"Isn't he beautiful!" Pocahontas would sigh. And his father would agree.

8

Lady Rebecca

John Rolfe had just returned from Jamestown. He was glad to be home. He tossed small Thomas up in the air and kissed Pocahontas.

"I have a surprise for you," he told her.

Her eyes shone like a child's. "Give it to me!" she begged.

Her husband laughed. He loved to tease her.

"I can't give it to you now. It is a trip to London. I must go there on business. I want to show my wife and son to my family and friends in England."

Pocahontas clapped her hands excitedly. "I must let my father know I am going away," she said.

It was not long before the Rolfes' ship set sail. Powhatan sent several Indian men and women with his daughter. She was a princess, and she must have a court.

The ocean voyage lasted many weeks. When they reached London, Pocahontas' eyes opened wide. She had never seen anything like it. The houses were very tall. Hundreds of people went about on foot, on horseback, or in carriages.

Pocahontas placed her hands over her ears. "This place is noisy."

Her husband smiled. "You will become used to it."

All of the Indians were amazed by the large city. Pocahontas could easily understand how one Indian brave felt. Powhatan had given him a long stick when he left Virginia. He told the man to cut a notch on it for every Englishman he saw. At first the Indian cut and cut, but soon he threw the stick away.

John Rolfe found a house for his family to live in. Each day he took his wife and little son out in their carriage. He wanted to show them everything.

People in London were eager to meet Pocahontas. She and John went to many fine parties.

They also went to the Globe Theatre to see William Shakespeare's plays. Pocahontas enjoyed the make-believe world of the stage. Perhaps her favourite play may have been *The Tempest,* for it was about the New World.

One day something very wonderful happened. Captain John Smith came to see her. She had not known that he was alive.

He was surprised by the changes in Pocahontas. He had left behind in Virginia a mischievous little Indian maid. Now he found a great lady whose name was on every tongue in London.

When Captain Smith came into the room, he bowed low in the usual English manner. Pocahontas was cold and distant and did not seem at all glad to see him.

"Have I offended you, my Lady Rebecca?" he asked. She turned aside. When she looked at him again, there were tears in her eyes.

"Once you called me Pocahontas, your Nonpareil," she told him. "Do you forget so quickly? For years I thought you were dead. Why did you not send me a message? Are you no longer my English father?"

"Indeed, I am," John Smith said. "I have never forgotten you. But the ocean is wide, and the years have passed quickly. When I met you today, I greeted you as an English gentleman greets a lady. But you will always be my Nonpareil—Without an Equal."

9

Pocahontas Longs
for Home

The carriage was waiting at the door.
Pocahontas and John Rolfe were about
to leave for Hampton Court. Pocahontas
was to be presented to the King and
Queen.

Pocahontas turned around so John
could see all sides of her gold and

scarlet gown. A high stiff lace ruff was about her neck. Long lace cuffs were at her wrists. In one hand she held a fan of ostrich feathers.

"Perfect!" John Rolfe said. "I must find an artist to paint your portrait."

Pocahontas bit her lip. "I am frightened, my husband."

"Nonsense," he replied. "You will be the most beautiful woman at court. Just remember who you are—Princess Pocahontas, the lovely daughter of King Powhatan."

He took her arm and helped her into the carriage. Soon they entered the gates of Hampton Court.

All the ladies and gentlemen at court stared at the Indian princess as she entered the great doors of the throne

room. At the far end of the room King James and Queen Anne waited to receive her.

Pocahontas made her way down the long aisle with courtiers on either side. There were admiring whispers as she passed.

"That proud head!"

"Those flashing eyes!"

"They call her 'the beautiful savage,'" one man said in a low voice.

His neighbour shook his head. "Beautiful—but not savage. She is a most gracious lady."

At last Pocahontas came near the raised dais where the King and Queen sat. She made a low curtsey as she had been taught.

Later the Queen gave Pocahontas a private audience. Pocahontas found it easy to talk to Queen Anne. She seemed almost like any other wife and mother.

"I knew all about you long before you came to court," the Queen told her visitor. "Captain John Smith wrote me a long letter about you even before you landed in England."

The Indian girl was startled. "I did not know that!" she exclaimed.

The Queen nodded. "He told me how you had saved his life, and that you had also saved Jamestown. He wanted to be certain you were well received in London."

Pocahontas could hardly believe her ears. She had fancied the captain cold and distant, and he had done all this for her.

Pocahontas and John spent happy months in London. But one day John Rolfe found his wife sitting quietly with her hands folded in her lap. She looked sad.

"What is wrong?" he asked anxiously. "It is not like you to be so quiet."

There were tears in her brown eyes. "I am homesick. I feel shut up in this great city. I want to go back to our plantation. I miss the wide rivers and the deep forests of my native land."

"So do I," her husband said. "As soon as I can find a west-bound ship, we will go home."

Pocahontas was happy again. In a few months she would see her father and her people. Little Thomas would not grow up a stranger to them.

At last, in 1617, the Rolfes boarded a ship for home. Pocahontas was not feeling well when they sailed. Before they were out of sight of land, she became very ill. John Rolfe insisted that the captain put into port at Gravesend.

Soon they discovered she had smallpox —a dreaded disease. Knowing that she would die, her last thoughts were of her two-year-old child.

"Take care of my little Thomas," she begged. "Let him grow up in the land where I was a child."

It was not long before she died and was buried in the churchyard at Gravesend. Broken-hearted John Rolfe set out once more with his small son for the New World. Soon the child became so ill that his father feared for his life. He turned back a second time and landed at Plymouth. There he left his son with a friend who promised to

send Thomas to his uncle, Henry Rolfe. Henry reared him like an English boy.

Thomas was a grown man before he came back to Virginia, where he married the daughter of an English settler. By then his father was dead. Thomas' children and his children's children, even down to the present day, have been proud of their Indian blood.

Every year now thousands of tourists visit a restoration of Jamestown in Virginia. There they may re-live the days of the first permanent English settlement in the New World. Foremost in their minds is the Princess Pocahontas. Three hundred and fifty years ago she showed that people of different race and colour can live together in peace and friendship.